This book is dedicated to my beloved Daddy, Virginia Tech Professor Emeritus H.P. Marshall (1925-2001), who took me to my first football game and ignited a life-long passion. And to my mother, the sweet southern lady who still morphs into a crazed Hokie fan when the whistle blows. And to my extraordinary children, Connor and Julianna, whose love and belief in me provide daily inspiration. And lastly, to my childhood girlfriends who share a special love for each other and the Hokies.

Sarah Marshall
Author and Co-Founder, Game Day Publications

To God, who has gifted me with the inspiration, passion, and abilities to dream big;
And to my loving family for giving me the support and patience needed to pursue those dreams.

Dan Steiner
Editor and Co-Founder, Game Day Publications

I dedicate this book to Jenn, Ava and Jax.

Matt Brown, Illustrator
www.mbrowni.com

Copyright ©2010, Game Day Publications, LLC. All rights reserved.

No part of this book may be reproduced by any means without permission of the publisher.

For more information please contact Game Day Publications at
www.gamedaypublications.com

For information regarding the CPSIA on this printed material call (203) 595-3636
and provide reference #RICH-31454.

Virginia Tech®, Hokies®, Virginia Tech Hokies®, and The Hokie Bird® are trademarks or registered trademarks of Virginia Tech and are used with permission.

ISBN: 978-0-9844399-0-4

Printed in China

LEARNING FOOTBALL
with THE HOKIE BIRD®

It's **GAME DAY** at Virginia Tech and Blacksburg is buzzing with fans, bands and excitement! Joe and his sister Emma woke up early today to decorate the car and drive to Lane Stadium with their Mom and Dad. Football is in the air and the whole family is fired up and ready to cheer for the Hokies!

Today the Hokies are playing a very tough team. But Joe and Emma have their *own* **BIG** problem. While they love *watching* football, sometimes they're confused because they don't really know how to *play* the game!

Joe and Emma decide they must find someone who can teach them how to play football before the game begins.

They see Dad grilling hamburgers and hot dogs for a group of happy Hokie fans at their tailgate party outside of the stadium and dash to his side. "Dad, Dad, can you teach us how to play football?" they beg.

"Sorry kids. But I've got lots of hungry Hokies to feed! I'll teach you *after* the game, OK?" says Dad as he flips another juicy hamburger.

Disappointed, Emma turns to Joe and says, "We'll never find anyone to teach us football before today's game starts."

Suddenly, a voice comes from behind their car. "Hey, kids!"

Emma looks up and sees the big wide grin of…**THE HOKIE BIRD!** Joe's mouth drops open as The Hokie Bird struts up to them and asks, "Anybody want to play football? I need to warm-up before the big game!"

"We do, we do!" chant Joe and Emma. "But Hokie Bird, we don't know *how* to play the game," they admit sadly.

"Hmmm," says The Hokie Bird stroking his chin. "I think I can help you with that – if it's alright with your Mom and Dad." The Hokie Bird turns, winks at Mom and Dad, and…

marches hand-in-hand with Joe and Emma into Lane Stadium. "Let's go learn some football, young Hokies!"

LESSON 1
The Object of the Game

The object of the game is to score more points than the other team. The team with the ball trying to score is called the **OFFENSE**. The team without the ball is called the **DEFENSE**. The team with the most points at the end of the game wins!

LESSON 2
The Offense

Teams on **OFFENSE** try to get the ball over the other team's **GOAL LINE** and score a **TOUCHDOWN**. They can also choose to **KICK** the ball through the other team's goal posts and score a **FIELD GOAL**. A touchdown is worth 6 points! A field goal is worth 3 points!

The **QUARTERBACK** is the leader of the **OFFENSE**. He calls the different running and passing plays. The player who runs the ball is called a **RUNNING BACK**. The player who catches the ball is called a **RECEIVER**.

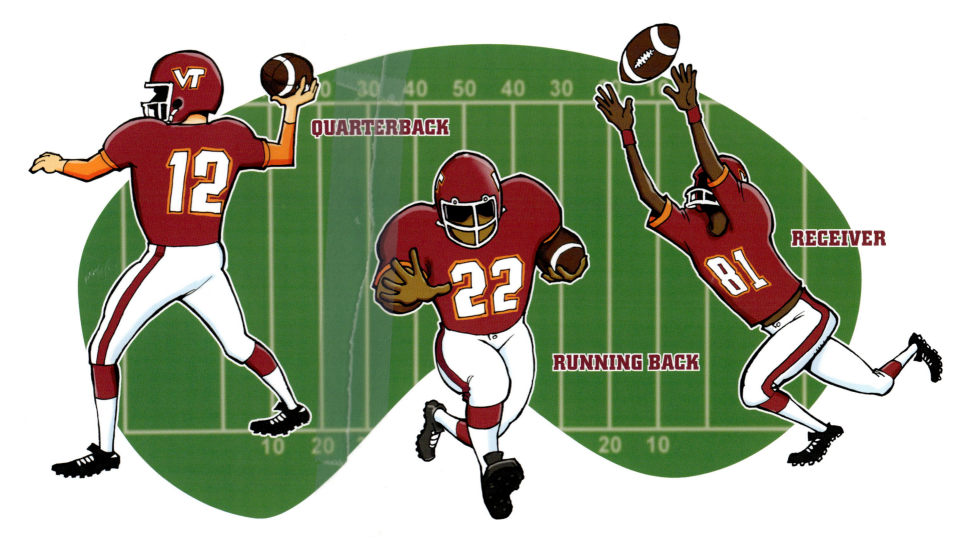

LESSON 3

The Four Downs

The **OFFENSE** gets 4 chances to gain 10 yards. Every time the offense gains 10 or more yards, they get a **FIRST DOWN** and 4 more chances to gain 10 yards. The offense wants to get as many first downs as possible, move the ball down the field, and **SCORE!**

LESSON 4

The Defense

The **DEFENSE** tries to stop the other team's **OFFENSE** from scoring points. The defense does this by **TACKLING** the other team's players when they have the ball. The defense tries to stop the offense from getting **FIRST DOWNS**.

The **DEFENSE** also tries to take the ball away from the **OFFENSE** by causing a **FUMBLE** or making an **INTERCEPTION**. The offense **FUMBLES** if they drop the ball. The defense can then take the ball away. If the defense catches a pass meant for the other team, they have **INTERCEPTED** the ball.

TACKLE   **FUMBLE**   **INTERCEPTION**

LESSON 5

The Officials

The people in the black and white striped uniforms are called the **OFFICIALS.** They are like the police, but for football. They make sure the teams follow all the **RULES** of the game. When a rule is broken, the officials throw a small yellow **PENALTY FLAG** onto the ground. The official then explains what **RULE** was broken and moves the ball in a way that penalizes the team that broke the rule.

Joe and Emma enjoyed their lesson and now know much more about football. As they are thanking The Hokie Bird, an announcement is made over the stadium speakers.

"What's that? Two officials are stuck in traffic and will miss the game? Oh, dear, I've got to think of something quick!" says The Hokie Bird as he paces the field.

Immediately, he turns to Joe and Emma and says, "It's an emergency and Virginia Tech needs your help! Will you take the place of the missing officials now that you understand the game? Are you up to the challenge, young Hokies?"

Joe and Emma high five each other and rush to The Hokie Bird's side and shout, **"We are ready!"**

The crowd is roaring and the big game begins. It's **KICK-OFF** time. Joe and Emma are wearing their black and white striped shirts and have yellow flags in their pockets. With "eagle-eyes," they watch every play to be sure no **RULES** are broken.

After an exciting afternoon of football, the game is now coming to an end. But the Hokies are losing by 2 points and there's only *one minute* left on the clock!

The Hokies have the ball and are marching down the field. They have just one more chance to score! With time running out, kicking a **FIELD GOAL** becomes their only option. But it's a *very* long kick…over 50 yards!

The coach searches the sideline and asks the team, "Who can kick the ball that far?!"

At that moment, The Hokie Bird trots onto the field! He's the team's best kicker with his big, strong legs. The fans cheer wildly as The Hokie Bird lines up for the kick. The clock is now down to *only* 5 seconds. As officials, Joe and Emma line up to make sure the ball goes **THROUGH** the goal posts.

BOOM! The Hokie Bird kicks the ball as hard as he can. The fans hold their breath as it sails through the air. Joe and Emma run onto the field to get the best view of the ball as it tumbles toward the goal posts.

"It's good!" shout Joe and Emma, their arms lifted high in the air signaling a successful kick. The fans in Lane Stadium cheer wildly, **"THE HOKIES WIN! THE HOKIES WIN!"**

The team rushes the field and lifts The Hokie Bird onto their shoulders! **VICTORY for the Hokies!** Joe and Emma stand to the side, happy for the win, but even happier they learned how to play the game of football.

As the celebration continues, The Hokie Bird looks down at Joe and Emma proudly and, as he tosses them the game ball, he asks, "Hey, kids, what are you doing *next* Saturday?"

HOKIE BIRD'S GAME DAY FOOTBALL GLOSSARY

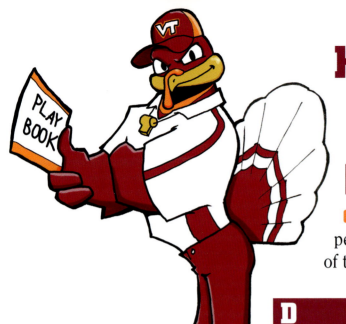

C
COACH — The person in charge of the team.

D
DEFENSE — The team without the ball that defends its goal and tries to stop the offense from gaining yardage.

E
END ZONE — This is the area where a player must enter with the football in order to score a touchdown.

F
FIELD GOAL — A place-kick that crosses over the bar and between the goal posts. A field goal scores 3 points.

FIRST DOWN
FIRST DOWN — The offense gets 4 tries to gain 10 yards. After 10+ yards are gained, the offense has made a first down and gets 4 more tries.

G
GOAL LINE — A line across each end of the field. When a team crosses the goal line they enter the end zone and a touchdown is scored.

K

KICKOFF — A place-kick from a tee that starts the game, the half, or after a team has scored.

O
OFFENSE — The team that has the football. The offense tries to cross the opponent's goal line by running or passing the ball.

HOKIE BIRD'S GAME DAY FOOTBALL GLOSSARY

OFFICIALS — The officials enforce the rules during a football game. They wear black and white striped shirts.

P

PENALTY — A punishment imposed on a team for breaking a rule.

PENALTY FLAG — The yellow flag which is thrown on the field by an official when a team or player has broken a rule.

Q

QUARTERBACK — The leader of the offense who calls the plays and takes the snap from center. The quarterback either hands the football off to a running back, passes to a receiver, or runs with the ball himself.

R

RECEIVER — The player who catches passes from the quarterback.

T

TACKLE — To bring a ball carrier down to the ground.

TOUCHDOWN — When one team crosses into the other team's end zone. A touchdown scores 6 points.

"OLD HOKIE" CHEER

**Hokie, Hokie, Hokie, Hy!
Tech, Tech, VPI
Sol-a-rex, Sol-a-rah
Poly Tech Vir-gin-ia
Ray rah VPI
Team! Team! Team!**